Crestwell School
P.O. Box 07159
Ft. Myers, Florida 33919
(239) 481-4478

Wishing you safe adventures!

Maryann Hurtt

NEPAL: A CHILDREN'S TRAVELOGUE

by

Maryan Hurtt

FIRST EDITION

UNIVERSITY EDITIONS, Inc.
59 Oak Lane, Spring Valley
Huntington, West Virginia 25704

Cover and interior art by the Author
Printed in Hong Kong

Dedication

My love and gratitude to my traveling companions, husband Caleb and son George for assisting me in organizing the material for this book. I am thankful for my daughter Kisa Harris, whose talent in graphic arts enabled her to give me much needed artistic advice. And, I am thankful for my daughter Dana's enthusiasm which helped this project along.

Our successful trip was led by Tom Laird of Wilderness Travel and assisted by Mountain Travel Nepal.

Foreword

Nepal is a small country far away in Asia. India, Burma, Tibet, & China are close neighbors. The capital of Nepal is Kathmandu which lies in the largest valley of the land. The country has a population of about 18 million. The majority of those people live, not in the cities, but in tiny villages that seem to blanket the hillsides. Since 1994, the governing body has been ruled by a Communist party. Nepal is officially a Hindu country, although the sherpas and most other high mountain people are Buddhists.

I trekked in this country during the spring of 1990 with my husband, Caleb, and our son, George. The experience was so rewarding, the scenery so amazingly beautiful, I wanted to share my impressions by using the drawings and photographs I did during the trip. This book is intended to introduce Nepal to elementary school children, and expand their desire to learn about other far away places.

This country has a gigantic mountain range that is along its northern borders called the Himalaya. This range extends from Assam in eastern India west to Afghanistan. It is a chain of the highest and youngest mountains on earth, including eight of the highest peaks known to man, Mount Everest being the highest at 29,028 feet. The Nepalese call this mountain "Sagarmatha," meaning "Head of the Seas." The Sherpas call it "Chomolungma," meaning "Goddess, Mother of the World."

Map of the World

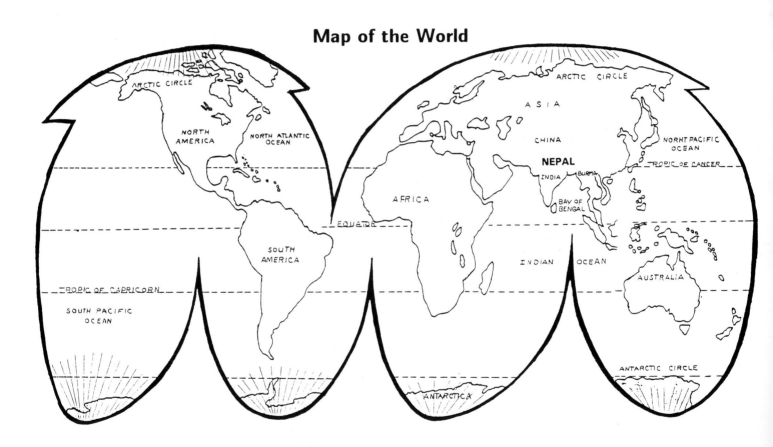

Map of the Trek We Are About to Take

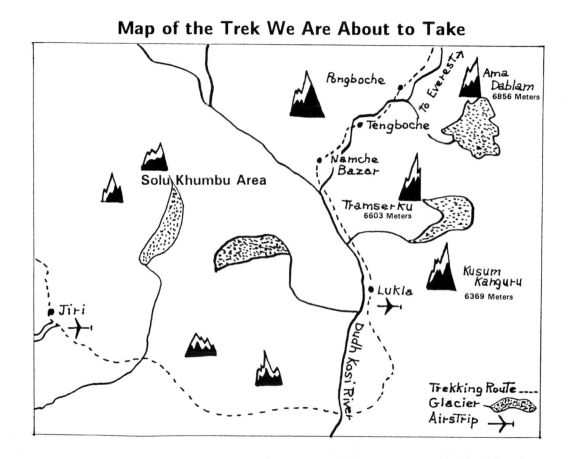

Flag of Nepal

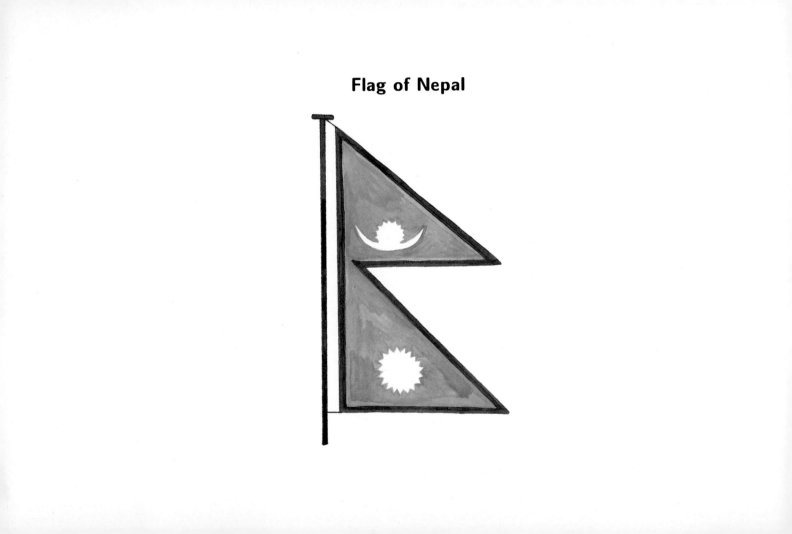

NEPAL: A CHILDREN'S TRAVELOGUE

We are going to fly on a Jumbo Jet to Nepal and trek into the Himalayan mountains to see Mt. Everest. Preparing for this trip you will need to find some space in your house so that you can spread out your gear as you collect it before packing your duffel bag.

You will need a passport and a Nepal visa that is good for three months . . . travelers checks, and a trekking permit.

Bring comfortable hiking boots, socks, shirts, pants, sweater, warm jacket, gloves, and a hat. Also, a day pack to carry your water bottle, camera, flash light, sun glasses, and rain gear. Don't forget your tooth brush, tooth paste, sun block, and other personal items.

Last but not least, be sure to bring your imagination and your energy.

We are planning this trip with a guide service that will supply us with tents, sleeping bags, food, a cook and porters to carry the supplies. You will need to be in good physical condition and consult your doctor for vaccinations you will need to protect your health.

A typical day of trekking will begin about 6 a.m. with tea brought to your tent. Breakfast consists of porridge and eggs or pancakes; milk, tea, or coffee. You will eat while the porters take down the tents and pack up the camp. The cooking crew will race ahead to find a good place to prepare lunch and wait for you. The afternoons are usually shorter ending about 4 p.m. when you round a bend to discover your tent is set up and some refreshments are waiting for you in the dining tent. Dinner is about 6 p.m. with some type of meat or chicken, not beef, as the cow is sacred to the Hindus. Rice or potatoes, noodles, a vegetable, some fruit and on special occasions, a cake or pie for dessert.

If your duffel bag is packed, let's be on our way and fly half way around the world to Kathmandu, the capital of Nepal.

Kathmandu is a large, spread out, bustling city of few good roads and a large outdoor market. Cows roam free through out the city and sometimes you can see an elephant with a man on his back, walking down the street. The city is a blend of the old and the new. Ancient carved temples surrounded by worshippers may have vegetable vendors and women laying out their laundry on the sacred steps.

There are two common religions in Nepal: Hinduism and Buddhism. The people's religious faith is very important in the way they live their lives. Where we will trek, most people are Buddhists. They believe that by doing good deeds today they may be rewarded with a good future later on. They love all living creatures and respect the majesty of the great mountains among which they live.

Here are some different forms of Buddha. One has a monkey on his lap. Buddha was a philosopher and teacher who lived before Jesus. Many of the Nepalese people try to live their lives according to his teachings. The eye in the middle of his forehead helps Buddha see everything.

Here are some icons or sculptured figures. The lotus blossom is a special flower and two of them are leaning against this sculpture.

During our trek we will often pass Mani stones. These slates have inscriptions hand carved on them and are piled high. The custom is to keep the structure on your right side as we pass by.

The prayer flags wave in the wind, sending out their messages to the people and the mountain gods.

We will see many religious structures that look like these monuments. The ones with the pointed tops are called CHORTENS. The structures with the painted faces and two eyes are called STUPAS.

What are some of the religious monuments called in our country?

We begin our journey by taking buses from Kathmandu to the small town of Jiri, where we will being our trek.

In 1953, Sir Edmund Hillary from New Zealand and Sherpa Tanzing Norgay from Tibet followed the route we are about to take on up to the summit of Mt. Everest, the first successful climb of this mighty mountain.

We meet the sherpa staff. The Sardar is the sherpa leader. Porters carry wicker baskets supported by a tumpline across their foreheads. You will be amazed at the amount of weight these people are able to carry. They will carry our gear up and down the mountain trails, do the cooking, and guide us to our destination.

The walking stick with a crossbar at the end may be used as a support during trekking or to lean against and sit upon while resting.

There are few roads in the high country, just narrow trails marking the routes up and down the mountain slopes. And, with the exception of a few airports, trekking is the only way you can travel or transport packages.

Can you name ways that we can travel in our country? How
is our mail carried?

Much of the land in the high country that is not too steep is cultivated. Looking across the valleys is very pretty seeing the terraces of crops growing. There are no tractors, all the work is done by hand or by oxen pulling a plow.

What kind of equipment do our farmers have to work with besides their hands?

Here we meet a porter resting his load against the wall. A girl walks by wearing tennis shoes that protect her feet. We wonder how the porters walk so well wearing flip-flops that have no support and are cold and slippery. We saw one who was bare footed and in the snow!

What are you going to wear on your feet when you come trekking?

We meet a woman sifting grain while her children play with Tibetan Mastiff puppies. The puppies are so fat and furry! They grow very large and help their masters herd animals and guard property.

As we head towards Mt. Everest, we trek in a region called the Solu Khumbu. There the houses are mostly made of stone. They have very few windows, to prevent drafts. Their only source of heat is an open fireplace where they also do the cooking. It's often very smoky in the house. To provide wood for the fireplaces, the great forests are being cut down.

The people must save their forests in order to prevent erosion of the soil and minimize landslides. The Nepalese need to find some other fuel as a source of heat, perhaps kerosene. But, there are many problems such as cost and back country transport, everything has to be carried on someone's back!

We meet a grandmom all dressed up in her best apron and wearing her pretty beads. The clothes she wears are very colorful.

Granddad is carrying one of his grandchildren. The older people take care of the children while the young parents work in the fields or are hired as porters.

Do your grandparents ever take care of you?

You can tell this grandmom is very proud of her grandchild . . . and even the duck seems delighted.

These people love their
animals and treat them with kindness.
Sometimes the animals share the houses by
living on the ground floor while the
people live on the second floor.

As we trek higher into these mountains we use less porters to carry our belongings and the loads are strapped to pack saddles on yaks. Zopyoks are also used. They are smaller animals and are the cross between a cow and the yak. The trails we follow are their highways. There are no roads, no cars, no trucks, no bikes, no rollerblades. We never ever see a wheel!

Here are some women securing a load on a zopyok. The ducks and chickens are enjoying the warm sun.

What animals have you seen being used to carry loads in our country?

These large animals with their long shaggy hair and big, sharp horns are the yaks. They are a very important domestic animal to these people. The yaks provide milk, wool, and are a source of food. Jewelry is even made out of the yak's bones. Their hides may be used for clothing and their dung is used for fuel to burn. The bells worn around their necks make a marvelous musical ring as they climb up and down the trails.

On the trails we often pass red robed men. They are monks . . . Buddhist clergy. They live in religious compounds, called monasteries, where they worship and do their daily chores.

Here we see a monk painting a decoration on a vase that will be placed in their temple.

What do you call your religious clergy? What special clothing do they wear?

The horses are small, but so are the people. Here is a woman dressed up wearing her jewelry. Her jewelry is probably very old and was passed to her through many generations. The horse is also dressed up and displaying a beautifully woven saddle blanket.

Do we as families ever pass our belongings on to other people or members of the family?

We pass by a male and female pheasant who are found living in the high country. The pheasant is the national bird of Nepal.

There are not many schools so the school children have to walk up and down the trails for several miles each day. These children have just passed by a pile of Mani stones to a lonely rhododendron tree that blooms in the spring with either red, pink, or white blossoms.

Do rhododendron trees grow in your country? How big do they grow? In Nepal they sometimes reach 60 feet in height!

The teacher is showing the children the location of Nepal in relationship to the rest of the world. Their closest neighbors are India and Tibet.

As we trek ever higher, our trail goes along a large rushing river. It is the Dudh Kosi . . . made up of Mt. Everest's melting snows. We often pass over this river on high swaying suspension bridges. They shake as we walk over them and it's best not to look down!

When we reach the end of the bridge we are "grateful" and spin the prayer wheel. The prayer wheel represents the cycle of life and death. As with the prayer flags, spinning the prayer wheel gives action to the religious messages written on the wheel.

There could be a big problem if you were passing over the bridge at the same time as a yak caravan was coming across. You could either turn and run or leap over the cable and hang on for "dear life" until they pass by.

As the trail starts a steep climb up to over 11,000 feet, we learn that we are coming to a village called Namche Bazar. Each Saturday there is an important weekly market, in which corn, rice, eggs, vegetables, and other items such as jewelry, rugs, and sweaters are sold. The food is carried to Namche Bazar from villages up to 10 days away!

It is an important social event as Sherpas from all the neighboring villages come to purchase goods and socialize with one another. Glad we didn't miss this day as it is an exciting market so high up in these awesome mountains and we can purchase some souvenirs for ourselves and friends.

Before entering some of the mountain villages, we might pass through a gateway. The ceiling and walls of these gateways are covered with beautifully hand painted religious symbols. The gateway is created to frighten away the evil spirits.

This design is a sample of the patterns on the ceiling of the gateway.

The next village we come to is Thyangboche, at 12,687 feet. From here we see a most magnificent mountain called Ama Dablam . . . looking like a sugar coated king sitting on a throne. Such a mountain! Trekking now at altitudes of 14,000 to 15,000 feet, we get snow showers instead of rain. The snow flakes cover our tents with fancy patterns and hang icicles off the edges. We go to the dining tent for a hardy meal, then rush back to our tents and climb into our bedrolls. In the morning we are awoken early by one of the porters serving us hot tea, cream and sugar. Then comes the hot water for washing. By the time we start our daily trek, we hope the snow on the trail will be melted.

In the snow, this porter is resting against his stick and has his wicker basket covered with plastic so the load he carries does not get wet.

These children have come to my tent to see if I might have any treats. They say, "NAMASTE" to me, which is a greeting to wish me a good day.

Finally, on a most beautifully clear day in the high altitude as our path leads us up around a corner, we see what we have come half way around the world to see, Mt. Everest! Though we have had glimpses of it before, now it towers up into the sky with much of it hidden behind the Lhotse-Nuptse wall. There is a contrail of blowing snow coming off the summit. To the right is Ama Dablam.

The yaks are not excited about reaching this destination, they are looking around for their hay, as at this altitude there is only rocks, dirt, snow and ice.

We have come a long way and it is time to head back down the mountains. But, you may stay if you like, to continue trekking and climb up to the summit of one of these great peaks.

Do people climb mountains in the U.S.? What is our highest mountain?

We will head down to Lukla, a little village at about 10,000 feet elevation. We have reservations to fly in a tiny airplane that carries only 14 or 15 passengers.

If the weather is bad there will be no flights. If flights are canceled we must wait for the backlog of people ahead of us to fly out first. The flight from Lukla to Kathmandu takes only 35 minutes while it took us many days trekking up and down the mountain passes from Jiri to Pangboche.

We do board the plane on the day of our scheduled departure and it was a bit scary as the runway seems so very short before the mountain just drops away as the plane reaches the cliff and soars up into the blue.

This seems like SHANGRILA! A nice hotel in Kathmandu, a hot shower, the first in over 2 weeks! We have a delicious lunch served to us in a lovely garden setting. As we sit there enjoying a cool drink, we wonder what far off land our journeys will take us to next.

About the Author

Maryan Hurtt was raised in a ranch family in Laramie, Wyoming. She attended the University of Wyoming and earned a B.A. degree from Bennington College in Vermont as an art major.

After college she lived in New York City and worked as a textile designer while studying at the Art Students League. She returned to the west, married and had a family of two girls, one boy, several horses, cows, various cats and dogs.

The author and her family are active outdoors people and have taken many trips to participate in physical activities. One of the most memorable was to Nepal in 1990, where the author made many sketches and took many photographs. The watercolors in this book are from that trip.